IS THERE A WAR ON SURBURBIA?

Is There a War on Surburbia?
Calling a Truce in the Battle Over Land Use

by Steven Greenhut

February 2025

ISBN: 978-1-934276-58-7

Pacific Research Institute
P.O. Box 60485
Pasadena, CA 91116
www.pacificresearch.org

IS THERE A WAR ON SURBURBIA?
CALLING A TRUCE IN THE BATTLE OVER LAND USE

By Steven Greenhut

VOLUME SEVEN

PR PACIFIC
RESEARCH
INSTITUTE

Are 'They' Coming for Our Suburbs?

CURRENT DEBATES OVER LAND-USE planning have taken on
the same strident, ideological and almost religious zeal that dominate other hot-button political disagreements, which isn't surprising
given that where we choose (or happen) to live reflects some of our
most fundamental values. Americans' politics are deeply divided by
cultural issues and there are few things more cultural than whether
we live in big cities: suburbia, small towns or the countryside.[1]

Politically, it's been true for decades that urbanites are more
likely to be socially liberal and supportive of Democratic candidates,
while rural areas and small towns are more conservative and trend
Republican. The suburbs have become a battleground, having shifted
from leaning Republican to leaning Democratic and back again in
the past few elections.[2] But when we parse the data, it's not always
clear what these distinctions really mean. The usual monikers often fall short.

For instance, the federal government had long defined a suburb based largely on county lines. So, as a 2020 Department of Justice report explained, the feds had classified all of San Bernardino
County, Calif. – the 20,105-square-mile county east of Los Angeles,
which is larger than the four smallest states combined – as a suburb.

Yet most of the county encompasses sprawling deserts and small towns. It includes genuine commuter suburbs, as well as a number of bigger cities and many uninhabited areas.[3]

In the Sacramento area, some "city" neighborhoods actually function like suburbs, with their quiet leafy streets dominated by single-family homes. Some of its suburbs, such as Roseville and Folsom, have significant downtowns.[4] One can find multi-family housing, mid-rise buildings and walkable communities throughout the region. Some "suburban" areas, such as Galt and Woodland, are home to many urban commuters, but really are notable for their small-town lifestyles. In Orange County, suburbs such as Irvine have high rises that rival those found in urban downtowns.[5]

These observations are backed by academic research. As Harvard University's Joint Center of Housing Studies explains, "The breadth of suburban diversity has been increasingly highlighted in recent decades by scholars and commentators. A growing focus on issues of inner-ring suburban decline in metropolitan areas like Cleveland and Baltimore and expanding suburban poverty across the country have stood in direct contrast to the traditional image of suburbia and have called into question the ways in which we define and conceptualize suburbs."[6]

This reinforces my view that many of our divisions tend to be overstated and unnecessary, that the cultural differences often are exaggerated. Furthermore, people live in different places at different times in their lives. My wife and I recently moved into an older section of a newer suburb, where we can walk to the Old Town. We left an acreage nearby. We previously lived in big cities, suburbs and small towns. Our values haven't changed, even as our living situations have.

That DOJ report found that inaccurate and arbitrary lines drawn between cities, suburbs and towns made it difficult for the agency to accurately understand crime data. Its new analysis revamped the criteria for determining a city, focusing instead on intra-county population density rather than county and municipal boundaries. That seems sensible. Its updated definitions conclude that, "12% of the population lives in urban areas, 69% in suburban areas, and 19% in rural areas."[7] Those are useful numbers for the purposes of this essay.

Back to this publication's title: Is there a war on suburbia? At first glance, it's hard to imagine government is waging a war on the lifestyle choice of 69% of the population. Yet the Independent Women's Forum argued that the Biden administration's fair-housing plan "is a radical plan that would crush the ability of American citizens to choose what kind of community in which to live." The article is unsurprisingly called, "Joe Biden's War on Suburbia."[8] One can find myriad articles that tout this theme, with the "war on suburbia" a common title.

According to that conservative women's group, the Biden plan used the concept of racial fairness to attack "local zoning laws, designed by local representatives, to create or preserve a town's density, leafiness, school quality and nature and location of commercial strips."[9] This is in essence a cultural argument. But now that President Donald Trump is back in office, we'll see how he intends to use the federal government's massive regulatory powers. His campaign offered some clues.

That talking point gained traction in the 2024 election. For instance, Trump posted on social media photos of a squalid African shanty town and implied that Democrats want to turn American suburbs into something similar. This wasn't a serious point, but an attempt to stoke fear in the suburban public. The meme echoes a more serious argument Trump and former Housing and Urban Development Secretary Ben Carson made in 2020, in *The Wall Street Journal* promising that, "We'll Protect America's Suburbs":[10]

> The crime and chaos in Democrat-run cities have gotten so bad that liberals are even getting out of Manhattan's Upper West Side. Rather than rethink their destructive policies, the left wants to make sure there is no escape. The plan is to remake the suburbs in their image so they resemble the dysfunctional cities they now govern. As usual, anyone who dares tell the truth about what the left is doing is smeared as a racist.

There's a lot to unpack in these sentences, some of it true and some of it not so much. But for starters, its approach doesn't recognize suburbia's demographic reality.

As demographer Wendell Cox wrote in a Free Cities Center article:[11] "Today, a majority of each large minority lives in the suburbs and exurbs, ranging from African-Americans (76.3%), to Asians (80.5%) to Hispanics (83.3%). These figures nearly equal the 90% of White-Non-Hispanics who live in the suburbs and exurbs." The supposed battle between cities and suburbs shouldn't take on racial or ethnic connotations. The suburbs are diverse. My large Sacramento suburb has a majority-minority population. A quarter of its residents are foreign born.

I raise the racial issue to defuse it. The real debate is about zoning, government regulations, subsidies and the quality of urban governance. Those issues are interrelated but different. There is in fact a concerted effort by progressives – based on an urbanist ideology that believes that car-centric living situations are environmentally unsustainable and destructive of our sense of community – to densify the suburbs. Some of their ideas, such as loosening zoning laws to allow higher-density construction, are perfectly consistent with free-market thinking. Others, such as subsidizing low-income housing projects and limiting single-family-home permits, are not.

In opposition to these policies, many conservatives (and some liberals in pricey growth-controlled areas such as Marin County, California, north of San Francisco)[12] argue that local governments are closest to the people and should have the power to determine local zoning and density rules and not be pre-empted by state and federal governments. State and federal subsidies for affordable-housing projects distort the marketplace and waste tax-payer dollars and the best way to solve the state's housing problems is by lowering taxes and regulations. Their latter argument often contradicts their earlier ones.

As noted above, many conservatives are stoking fear by using the kind of culture-war imagery promoted in Trump's social-media post and op-ed. But many urbanist progressives also make an over-heated cultural argument that falsely depicts modern suburbia as the epitome of racially segregated, patriarchal 1950s-era America, where oppression, discrimination and classism rule the day. It's almost as if the people who make these arguments have rarely ventured out of their hip urban neighborhoods – or haven't realized how much the suburbs have changed in the past half century.

They often are forthright about their goals, many of which understandably concern suburbanites. It's easy to find screeds decrying the supposed evils of suburbia. This is from *Medium*:[13] "The American Dream is dead and I'm glad it's gone. Americans have been obsessed with obtaining their slice of the 'picturesque' suburban pie that has defined modern America for 70 years. But as we're finding out, this lifestyle is unsustainable, and the consequences of this failed suburban experiment have grown into an uncontrollable monster that is destroying our country's stability."

Here's an example from *Quartz*:[14]

(I)t's been difficult to elucidate in specific physical terms what it is about suburbia that makes it so hostile to humanity. To someone with no training in architecture, it's often experienced as a great, non-articulated existential malaise, like depression. You know it sucks, but it's hard to say exactly why … It's telling that we have no widespread cultural vernacular for why classical urban settlements … are pleasant. It's because Americans took that inheritance and unceremoniously discarded it, consonantly with the rise of the mass-produced automobile. … (M)any of us know, on some level, that we live in a dystopian nightmare but can't say what makes it a dystopian nightmare.

New master-planned communities, tract neighborhoods and look-alike shopping centers might not be everyone's cup of tea, but dystopias? On the other hand, many conservatives have used real-world urban problems such as homeless encampments, retail crime rings and open-air drug markets to depict big cities as dangerous wastelands.[15] Those problems are real, but the targeted cities mostly are safe, attractive and orderly. Despite their poor governance, cities such as San Francisco, Portland and Seattle are not 1970s Detroit.

So the battle lines are drawn: conservatives who want to protect our current living arrangements v. progressives who want to use the government to upend them. But not so fast. This is where a depiction of this "war" is lacking in nuance. For starters, we need to recognize that American suburbs themselves were largely the fruit of government zoning and planning. Many critiques of suburbia come not just from progressives, but from free-market advocates who realize that many urbanist reforms reduce government rather than expand it.

Another prime conservative complaint is that states are undermining local zoning and other authorities. In California and Oregon, for instance, the legislatures have essentially eliminated single-family-only zoning by overriding local restrictions on Accessory Dwelling Units, duplexes and multi-family housing. (Note: I always refer to it as single-family-*only* zoning rather than single-family zoning because builders are still allowed to build single-family homes.)[16] As we've explained at the Free Cities Center, mixing multi-family housing with single homes doesn't necessarily diminish the neighborhood and often enlivens it with architectural and lifestyle variety.

The end goal ought to be more freedom and a broader protection of property rights. When conservatives trot out the "local control" argument, they're mainly arguing over which branch of government is most entitled to regulate one's life. In other areas of policymaking (taxes, gun control, rent control, business regulations), conservatives have been leading a "pre-emption" movement that encourages states to limit the power of the locals. Yet when land uses are at issue, they suddenly treat local control as the nation's fundamental governing principle. As I wrote in *The Orange County Register*:

> Local control isn't a principle, but a practical way to evaluate the proper level of government to undertake basic functions. Obviously, local governments are closer to the people and are the proper arm to fill potholes. You

wouldn't want to depend on far-off bureaucrats to do that. The goal of conservatism is not to assure that a local bureaucrat is the one to erode your property rights. The real principle is the advancement of freedom.[17]

I was writing about the suburban city of Huntington Beach. Its conservative-controlled City Council continues to challenge state housing laws that reduce zoning hurdles and force growth-averse cities to permit more housing development. Ironically, the city's lawsuit against the state trots out the same environmental and no-growth arguments long common among progressives. The state has been heavy handed in its enforcement, but it's mind blowing watching progressive state officials call for fewer regulations while conservative local ones – using the local-control argument, of course – call for stricter enforcement of them.[18]

However – and this is an important caveat – most urbanists only are interested in reducing government to the degree that such reductions lead to their desired goal of higher densities. They are unreliable allies at best. They tout deregulation, but then try to stop the spread of suburbia by, say, opposing new housing projects that are designed as low- or mid-density suburbs.

They rely on government subsidies to promote the construction of multi-family housing, even though market-rate developers often build these projects less expensively without the red tape. A recent *Wall Street Journal* article found that a Los Angeles developer was able to build affordable housing for roughly half the cost after it decided to eschew subsidies.[19] My goal is fewer regulations and freer markets, while theirs is urbanization and density.

Furthermore, urbanists typically support inclusionary zoning and other government mandates that force developers to set aside a portion of their new developments at under-market prices – something that drives up the overall cost and only benefits a few lucky people who figuratively (and sometimes literally) win the lottery.

And they really dislike the private automobile and lobby to reduce traffic lanes, stop freeway expansions and divert increasing shares of transportation revenues toward underused (and frequently mismanaged) transit systems and bike lanes. Much of the urbanist advocacy comes from young ideologues who prefer mockery ("car-brained suburbanites!") to constructive solutions – and who seem unaware or uninterested in the living needs of people with children or at least anyone at a different stage of life than them or who have different preferences.

Urbanists also frequently ignore the one salient point made by Trump and Carson.[20] Current city governments typically do an atrocious job handling the basic public-safety, infrastructure and educational needs within their jurisdictions. Those reasons include union domination of City Hall and the liberal tilt of urban governments and bureaucratic inertia. Instead of improving urban governance and services (which means taking on vested interests, including their progressive political allies), urbanists seem most committed to coercing people to live in these places by reducing the number of new developments outside the urban footprint.[21] They rarely take seriously ideas that would, say, privatize certain services.

My argument in this booklet is that the issue isn't entirely black and white, that we need not choose sides in a cultural debate between cities and suburbs. I'm a fan of cities, suburbs, towns and rural areas. They all have their charms, offer choices and are a crucial part of the nation's cultural fabric. I have family members who live in big cities, small towns and suburbs. Why do I have to choose sides? Instead, we should promote market-based policies – reducing regulations, loosening the iron grip of zoning, allowing private developers to meet various consumer niches – that make all places better places. There certainly is a middle ground provided policy-makers and ideologues stop trying to dictate the "best" living arrangements for everyone.

For instance, instead of replacing the old, rigid suburban building codes with new, rigid urbanist codes, perhaps local leaders "should not neglect the possibility that the incremental deregulation of certain land uses might prove more advisable," wrote Nicole Stelle Garnett in the *Yale Law Review*. "Ultimately, permissive land use reforms in our cities, rather than prohibitory ones in our suburbs, may represent the best hope for urban regeneration."[22] That's music to my ears.

As noted earlier, some suburban areas have vibrant downtowns. There's no reason we can't achieve both goals: making suburbs more appealing and walkable, and making cities safer and more accessible for broader swaths of the public. Instead of viewing it as a war, perhaps we should view the issue as a conflict that's ripe for creativity, compromise and negotiation.

Two Cheers for the Suburbs

BEFORE WE CONSIDER ANY WAR on suburbs, it's best to define suburbia beyond the statistical determinations used by federal bean counters – and beyond the stereotypes. The definition seems obvious at first glance. The term is Latin, with "sub" meaning close and "urb" meaning city.23 Suburbs are predominantly residential. Most residents commute to other parts of the urban area, often downtown. Modern suburbs typically are car-dependent. Residential areas are separated from other land uses, such as commercial, retail, educational and religious. They often include gated communities. They feature strip-style shopping centers along commercial routes.

There's not much more to it than that. There's great variety from early 20th century streetcar suburbs to modern master-planned communities with sprawling mini-mansions and a plethora of parks and trails. As I explained in my previous Free Cities Center booklet, "Building Cities from Scratch,"24 every city was once a new city. Charming historic big-city neighborhoods – consider the sea of brick row homes in Philadelphia or Victorians in San Francisco – were master planned along the standards of the time. They were built on empty lots or farm fields and often on a large scale, similar to

modern suburban neighborhoods. Older master-planned communities – at least those dating to the 1970s and 1980s – expressed the
best practices of urban thinkers at the time.

Some of the most interesting urban neighborhoods originally
were suburbs. It's just that the metropolitan area grew so much that
they now are part of the urban core. One main urbanist rap against
suburbs is that they are soulless, look-alike and boring. But over time,
the trees grow, owners paint and add on to their properties, and suburban neighborhoods can become settled and even interesting. They
can become even more interesting if we loosen zoning's straitjacket,
but they aren't all soulless. There are plenty of uninteresting suburbs
and lots of interesting ones, too. Urban neighborhoods can also be
drab or exciting. Many urbanists dislike suburbs based on matters of
aesthetics and taste, even if they bolster their anti-suburban diatribes
with warnings about climate change and social isolation.

The more serious, less-subjective critiques are that because of
their rigid zoning, they are unable to change to meet new needs
– and that they necessitate the use of private automobiles to par-
ticipate in virtually every daily activity. That's largely true. Urbanists
also argue that suburbs promote racial and economic segregation,
but that's largely false. As noted previously, the numbers show that
suburbs often are more multi-cultural and diverse than big cities.
Increasingly, major cities have become the province of the wealthy
and poor, young professionals and retirees. The lack of space, safe
parks and good schools has turned cities such as San Francisco and
Seattle (more on that later) into virtually childless cities. Many of
the hippest city neighborhoods are remarkably lacking in diversity,
as they are the playground of young, urban professionals.[25]

My conclusion is that urbanists simply don't like suburbs because
they don't appeal to their senses. They place a higher value on, say,

the ability to walk to a cool new coffee shop or bar than they do on convenience, a sense of cleanliness and safety, and the pleasures of having a yard, garage and abundant living space. The city neighborhoods where people can have the latter are notable mainly because they originally were built as suburbs. And those areas typically are not attainable even for dual-income middle-class people in major West Coast cities. You need around $1.5 to $2 million to afford a row house in some of San Francisco's outer districts. Everyone is free to have their own preferences, but urbanists often use policy tools to foist their preferred design on the public.

A study by the Pew Research Center found that suburbs are enjoying the most population growth in the country: "Suburban and small metro counties have grown since 2000 because of gains in all the drivers of population change. They gained 11.7 million new residents by drawing former residents of U.S. urban and rural areas, as well as immigrants from abroad. On top of that, they had 12.1 million more births than deaths."[26] Unlike in cities, suburbanites are having children in significant numbers. And, per Pew, the suburbs are more economically diverse than ever. Although urbanism is the rage in academia and elite media, the suburbs remain the most-popular living choice for Americans. Yet that doesn't soften all the handwringing, most of it based on caricatures of suburban living.

"The trouble with the suburbs is that big houses with big yards, set behind wide streets and long driveways, make socializing much harder," wrote Chris Weller in *Business Insider*. "And since everyone is driving from A to B, unlike in large cities were residents walk or take public transportation everywhere, people who live in the suburbs have to make a much more active effort to socialize."[27]

Personally, I've found this to be incorrect. Because people have such limited private space and are far more likely to be renters and therefore are more transient, big-city neighborhoods tend to be the least friendly ones I've lived in. It's not unusual to have never met the person living in the apartment next door. In the suburbs, people have plenty of interior space and backyards. They more frequently are owners and settled in the community. As a result, they typically – and this is admittedly based solely on my experience – are friendly. And I've never heard of any regular public-transit rider say that buses and trains offer great chances to socialize.

Community is what you make it. Architecture and land use obviously have an impact on our human interactions, but no planning concept offers a simple solution to promote a sense of community. That's up to us as individuals. Indiana-based writer Andrew Smith debunked the "suburbs lack community" argument in a column for the Free Cities Center:

> While suburbs are often considered devoid of community, the opposite is true. Community bonds are often forged around churches and religious organizations, and because suburban communities by their nature tend to cater to families with children, the school becomes the epicenter of that community. In my community, we felt welcomed almost immediately by seeing neighbors on our daily walks around the neighborhood, but even more so by those we attend church with and see every Sunday, and forge even greater bonds at the Friday night high school football and basketball games.[28]

Despite the truths here, it's increasingly hard to find anyone in popular media or academia to defend the communities that most of us call home. So there is indeed an ideological war on suburbia going on. The big question is whether the policies that urban policy types advocate pose a real threat to suburbanites – or whether some of them might actually make suburbia better. It's hard to argue, for instance, that the creation of more walkable retail areas, nicer parks, more sidewalks and better bike lanes pose a threat to the suburban way of life. I'd say they enhance it.

The modern tract-house suburb has its roots in post-World-War II America. Many of modern suburbia's strongest defenders depict suburban communities as a bastion of freedom and private enterprise. Suburban living does in fact provide many personal freedoms, such as the ability to own a home, jump in the car and go wherever one pleases regardless of the transit schedules. But the foundations of these communities were built by the federal government in the form of federally backed mortgages, the construction of the Interstate Highway System and the G.I. Bill, which provided home and college subsidies to those returning from the war.

In the post-war era, the nation faced a massive housing crunch, as explained by a piece published by the State University of New York (SUNY):

> Suburban neighborhoods of single-family homes tore their way through the outskirts of cities. William Levitt built the first Levittown, the archetype suburban community, in 1946 in Long Island, New York. Purchasing mass acreage, "subdividing" lots, and contracted crews to build countless homes at economies of scale, Levitt offered affordable suburban housing to veterans and their families. Levitt became the prophet of the new suburbs, heralding a massive internal migration. The country's suburban share of the population rose from 19.5% in

1940 to 30.7% by 1960. Homeownership rates rose from 44% in 1940 to almost 62% in 1960.[29]

Expanded homeownership rates and suburban living fueled the post-war economic boom, it added: "As manufacturers converted back to consumer goods after the war, and as the suburbs developed, appliance and automobile sales rose dramatically. Flush with rising wages and wartime savings, homeowners also used newly created installment plans to buy new consumer goods at once instead of saving for years to make major purchases."[30]

Social critics will always look nostalgically at life in dense urban settings, but that life was typically overcrowded, impoverished and dirty. Elite planners in the 1950s sought to eliminate what they often viewed as soul-depleting slums. The new suburbs might have offered a sanitized life – and there's no question that early suburban neighborhoods sadly often were segregated by law – but it's a life that huge numbers of Americans willingly embraced. It led to economic growth, rising wages and a notable increase in homeownership rates, which have long been a path to wealth creation for the middle and working classes. Most of those outcomes are praiseworthy.

So why only two cheers for suburbia?

This new form of planning did in fact change the traditional neighborhood structure of the nation. We gained many good things, but lost some good ones as well. As a result, a new movement was born to create communities that are based on older planning concepts. It's called the New Urbanism. Smart Growth[31] is the term for that movement's planning arm. And both ideas have intersected with a politically successful Yes In My Back Yard (YIMBY) movement designed to promote housing construction, mainly of the multi-family variety. Virtually every planning and ar-chitecture school in the nation promotes urbanism as the desired goal, so it's no surprise so many energetic young urbanists have be-come so outspoken. Many of them grew up in suburbs and are well aware of their flaws. They often live in cities and love urban life.

Yet the results of this movement are a mixed bag, with some urbanists mainly trying to upgrade the quality of suburban living, while others do indeed seem committed to wiping away the subur-ban option. Let's take a look at this new movement that's based on old concepts.

The Good, Bad and Ugly of Suburbia

THE BASIC PREMISES of the New Urbanist movement took shape in the early 1990s. One of its founders, Andrés Duany, pointed to what I see as the good aspect of it: "The New Urbanism began as essentially market-oriented, when, after Seaside, it turned out many people wanted to live in walkable, diverse places and the developers were not yet providing them."[32] Many people desire to live in traditional communities and developers ought to be free to build them. Seaside, Fla., remains a highly coveted destination, although it's largely a playground for the wealthy – hardly an example of economic or social diversity.[33] More recently, the California Forever project in northern California seeks to build an entirely new and economically diverse city based closely along New Urbanist lines. Bravo.

However, Duany added that in the movement's second phase its supporters "bonded with NIMBYism as part of the solution and not part of the problem as we, too, were critical of conventional development." This is not so good. The Not In My Back Yarders "wanted no more of the traffic and imbecilic development. They could not precisely identify the problem, but instinctually hated it."[34] In essence, urbanists and no-growthers made common cause to stop new "sprawl" development, which helped lead to the housing shortages of the last decade, especially in California, Oregon and Washington.

The movement's latest phases have resulted in some of the ugly "war on suburbia" rhetoric: "The third phase was driven by health concerns," Duany added. "It began with the scientific proof that the sedentary and socially isolated lifestyle required by sprawl caused problems for both physical and emotional health. The fourth phase coincided with the emergence of environmentalism as the principal political movement of our time. The New Urbanism, with its compact, walkable, transit-ready patterns, is inherently sustainable, and integral to the environmental movement."[35]

By tying urban design to public health activism and environmentalism, the New Urbanists shifted from a design philosophy to an ideological crusade that was eager to use government to stop the "bad" soul-destroying, health-eroding, climate-change-promoting suburban lifestyle and replace it with the "good" kind of development that promotes happiness and sustainability. When presented as such a stark choice, there's little room for my preference: letting the market provide various types of communities, with individuals choosing the ones that best suit them. (As an aside regarding health, a recent study shows that, "Living in a big city certainly has its perks, but research suggests that air and noise pollution and a lack of green spaces can be detrimental to our health and well-being," according to *Discover*.)[36]

Not only leftists decry the suburban model. Although his politics are hard to pinpoint, novelist and social critic James Howard Kunstler has received a receptive audience for his attacks on suburbia from the right, especially from paleo-conservatives. Kunstler is well known for promoting the peak-oil theory, which argues that oil production eventually will plummet and obliterate our oil-dependent economy – sending it to pre-industrial conditions. Part of his argument is that the nation needs to change its living patterns before that disaster strikes. He is a fellow at *The American Conservative*, which says he "might best be described as a patriot for an America that no longer exists: a country of small towns, tight-knit communities, human-scale development and local entrepreneurship."[37]

Kunstler, who calls for rebuilding the nation in a more traditional, human-scale urban form, summarized his views of suburbia:

> The National Automobile Slum and all its accessories represent a titanic mis-investment of our national wealth, and we are now stuck with an inventory of physical structures that will be impossible to maintain and may be of little utility in the future. ... The asteroid belts of suburban tract developments and highway commerce that surround every town in America, big and small, are disintegrating as we speak. I get calls every week from reporters around the country who want to know what happens to dead shopping malls. ... Personally, I believe it will take a severe economic and/or political shock to the United States for us to really, seriously change our behavior and the value system that supports our behavior. I believe this shock is coming soon—and, not-so-ironically, it will be a consequence of our foolish mis-investments in malls, theme parks and drive-thru fry-pits.[38]

I quote Kunstler not only because he is pithy, but because he epitomizes the tendency of urbanists to depict the current situation in catastrophic and judgmental terms – and fail to see the obvious solutions to problems that they identify. For instance, he was prescient about the plight of shopping malls. His quote was from 1999 and malls have died in massive numbers since then. But the solution might not require the complete re-ordering of society or economic collapse that he predicts. Instead, our state and cities are simply rezoning them for other uses.[39] Developers are capable of adapting old buildings for new uses. Perhaps the solution is loosening government land-use restrictions to enable them to do so.

To the degree that modern government planners seek to use force to create different land-use patterns, they are indeed waging a war on suburbia. But to the degree that they simply remove old restrictions and allow new forms to emerge, they are doing no such thing. Critics of proposed land-use changes need to make this important distinction, but too often they just choose a side in the battle and claim that their foes are trying to destroy their suburban communities.

Lawmakers are, of course, doing both things, good and bad. Portland, Ore., remains the New Urbanist nirvana, as in 1979 it imposed an urban-growth boundary that restricts development outside of its arbitrarily drawn green line.[40] The goal was to stop urban sprawl and protect agricultural land. The Metro agency that controls it occasionally expands its size to allow for additional construction, but the process is rigid. Australian cities have embraced similar New Urbanist concepts and conduct limited land releases to allow for new development. That country is the size of the continental United States, but has only 27 million people v. the U.S.'s 334 million and tightly restricts growth outside of its handful of urban centers.[41] Wherever they are implemented, growth boundaries limit construction and drive up home prices. They also have largely failed to achieve their stated objective of stopping sprawl.

As *Market Urbanism*'s Scott Beyer writes about Portland in *Forbes*:

> While it is true that when passing many parts of the growth boundary, the land shifts instantly from urbanization to beautiful countryside, a further drive reveals that a lot of the growth is just further extending. For example, two of Oregon's four fastest-growing cities are small ones – Sandy and Canby – that sit about 10 miles beyond the growth boundary. Just north of Portland, across the Columbia River and outside the UGB (Urban Growth Boundary), is Vancouver, which is routinely one of Washington State's fastest-growing cities. Since 1990, its population has nearly quadrupled from 46,000 to 173,000, and it too has fast-growing northern suburbs. And Salem, 60 miles to the south, has shown formidable growth recently also.[42]

Many California regions also have imposed urban-growth boundaries, with similar results of higher prices, leapfrog developments and even longer commutes. One of the common arguments in favor of denser living is its supposedly lower carbon footprint. That's debatable, as some studies suggest that denser communities cause the most climate harm. But even if it is true, it hardly helps the environment if home buyers simply move farther out to afford their dream home. The San Francisco Bay Area has large numbers of "super commuters" precisely because its sky-high home prices send commuters over the Altamont Pass into Central Valley farm regions in search of affordable houses.[43]

By contrast to these counterproductive growth regulations, the California Legislature has in recent years passed a number of zoning reforms that deserve praise from free-market advocates. A series of new laws have legalized the construction of ADUs and created "by right" approval processes (allowing developers to bypass planning commission and city council hearings) that streamline approvals. Property owners gain the right to build their project without subjective reviews provided they follow the local planning standards regarding setbacks, lot sizes and the like. New laws also up-zone (allowing more types of projects to be built) areas along transit corridors to allow streamlined construction of higher-density apartments and condos.

Of particular note, California Senate Bill 9,[44] which went into effect in January 2022, lets homeowners build two duplexes on a property currently zoned for a single-family home, a measure that essentially eliminates single-family-only zoning that banned those multi-family projects. The law was overturned by a lower court, but the state is challenging that ruling. Data this year shows that the law was only having a modest effect on the state's housing stock with only a few hundred permits pulled to build them, but it nevertheless is a sensible, market-oriented solution. Such reforms take time to bear fruit. More than 80,000 ADUs have been built in the state since California legalized them in 2016.[45] But much more needs to be done, including broader efforts to de-regulate land uses.

The lackluster results of the latest laws reflect the high costs of construction in California and the limited number of properties with large enough lots to take advantage of the reforms. In addition, local governments often drag their feet on approvals or file lawsuits challenging the legislative changes. These are non-coercive ways to achieve the goals of higher density. It is absurd when government regulations forestall the conversion of old shopping malls and low-density strip malls into higher-value uses.

Yet, critics of the reforms continue to tout the "war on suburbia" theme even for these deregulatory approaches. Writing for the California Policy Center, Edward Ring (who also occasionally writes for the Free Cities Center and was featured in one of its videos), warns against "California's Progressive War on Suburbia" and uses, as evidence, that the state has "attempted to legislate high density housing by taking away the ability of cities and counties to enforce local zoning laws."[46]

Ring's article raises many salient points that we often make in the Free Cities Center. As he notes, the state needs to reform the California Environmental Quality Act (CEQA), which imposes costly burdens on housing and other types of construction. The state provides costly housing subsidies that provide artificial incentives to urbanize suburban communities.[47] And he says California regulations are the key reason for our unaffordability crisis. He's right on those points, but we shouldn't lump deregulation bills in the "war on suburbia" narrative.

For urbanists and their critics alike, markets – allowing builders to create the kind of communities that address varied consumer demand – should be the first-reach answer, not something to be used only as a means to achieve one's desired results. If one land-use system is preferable to another, then people will willingly choose it. There's plenty of evidence that many people would choose more walkable neighborhoods if they were available and affordable.[48] So let's make it easier to build them without making it harder to build other types of neighborhood.

The Ongoing War on Cars

AS URBANISTS RECOGNIZE, the entire suburban enterprise would not be possible without the automobile. As a report for the National Bureau of Economic Research explained in 2004, "In 1910 the average American city was a small and densely populated place and less than one percent of Americans owned a car. By 1970, almost every family in the US owned at least one automobile."[49] I don't see the point in behaving like a Luddite who tries to contain the spread of a transformative invention, but urbanists continue to complain about cars.

The original suburbs, the report added, sprung up in the 1870s – driven, so to speak, by the creation of streetcar (rail) systems. Notably, "modern" light-rail systems are designed to recreate that approach. But technology moves along and the assembly line production of cars – combined with rising incomes – "encouraged movement to less dense areas where housing was more affordable."[50] Again, urbanites also fled the often-squalid conditions in bigger cities.

As much as modern urbanists love to attack the suburbs, they save their harshest critiques for automobiles. Go onto any urbanist social-media group and you'll find frequent references to "car-brained suburbanites," "death machines" and lots of commentary about the escalating size of American vehicles.[51] They raise some valid points. It is strange that full-size pickup trucks are the nation's top-selling vehicles and most of them apparently are used as basic family conveyances. They pose increasing dangers to pedestrians. Vehicle fatality rates fell to a five-decade low point of around 35,000 annually in 2015 and have risen to 41,000 in 2023 in conjunction with the growing mass of new vehicles.[52] Still, their anti-car fixation seems counterproductive.

Ultimately I believe that people should be free to drive whatever vehicle they choose. It's not outrageous to suggest that our communities offer reasonable alternatives to cars, but the urbanist movement seems committed to car-bashing – blaming them for every conceivable social ill and penning rants about their impact on the climate. Even their transit promotion is misguided, as they rarely wrestle with the reality that our current transit systems are overly costly, often dingy and plagued by crime. They fail, as my previous Free Cities Center booklet explained,[53] to put customers first. Then they wonder why potential customers avoid buses and rail systems that aren't convenient and don't accommodate cross-suburb commuters.

There is arguably a war on cars, not just from urbanists but from many regulators and legislators, especially in California and other blue states. Just as one can find endless anti-suburban screeds in various places, one can find even more heated denunciations of the automobile and its impact on society. Too often, car critics refuse to acknowledge the benefits that private vehicles offer. They yammer about the high cost of cars but ignore that many workers, especially in the building industry and trades, go to myriad jobsites and can't depend on suburb-to-city transit.[54] Cars are expensive, of course, but they still are cost effective as they allow people to live in less-expensive areas and avoid the pricey private-school tuitions needed in big cities with poor-performing school districts. Every invention has costs and benefits, but it's hard to argue with ideologues who pretend to know what's best for their fellow citizens and propose draconian solutions.

"Let's abandon this disastrous experiment, recognize that this 19th-century technology is now doing more harm than good, and plan our way out of it. Let's set a target to cut the use of cars by 90% over the next decade," wrote *Guardian* columnist George Monbiot. "Yes, the car is still useful – for a few people it's essential. It would make a good servant. But it has become our master, and it spoils everything it touches. It now presents us with a series of emergencies that demand an emergency response."[55] Unlike many anti-car activists, he at least admits that cars can be useful.

Obviously, cars aren't going away any time soon, and certainly not within a decade, but urbanists and climate warriors are increasingly proposing far-fetched proposals that will impede our lives. As is always the case, policymakers will try to implement some of these ideas on a smaller scale. It's a trend in Europe to try to ban cars from downtown areas or even wide sections of cities. The city of Berlin is attempting to ban driving from an area larger than all of Manhattan.[56]

The German transportation secretary in April proposed banning car use on weekends throughout the country and imposing much-lower speed limits all the time as a means to battle climate change.[57] Such ideas have run up against what commentators refer to as Germany's car culture,[58] as the nation has higher car-owner-ship rates than elsewhere in Europe and a history of automobile manufacturing with iconic companies such as Volkswagen, BMW and Mercedes.

California also is known for its car culture, but that hasn't stopped our legislators from attempting to dramatically reduce car usage. We've seen efforts to reduce car access on some downtown streets, as well as road diets that limit car lanes in downtown areas.[59] It's infuriating that the latter often are funded by a law that promised to reduce congestion. In this country, these arguably are small annoyances and are sometimes justifiable. Limiting an occasional downtown street to pedestrians can be useful. And no free-market supporter should complain about the privately funded developments that ban car use. If consumers want to make that choice, there's nothing wrong with offering it – provided it's not mandated or subsidized.

More significantly, California announced a ban on the sale of new internal-combustion vehicles starting in 2035, but many anti-car warriors aren't particularly interested in seeing consumers switch from gas cars to electric vehicles.[60] "EV production is unsustainable. EV batteries are composed of several rare earth minerals, including cobalt and lithium," according to an article last year in *Chicago Policy Review*. Mining companies expose nearby communities to high levels of toxins that are especially harmful to children." Instead of promoting EVs, the author argues that "sustainable mass transit should be the central U.S. transportation policy solution to fight climate change."[61] By the way, Trump already has signed an executive order unwinding Biden-era EV targets.

Yet that critique touches on the central problem for the anti-car crowd. Western states in particular have been investing heavily in transit infrastructure. The Southern California Association of Governments (SCAG) has found that despite massive decades-long investments in Los Angeles region transit systems, transit ridership continues to fall precipitously: "The most significant factor is increased motor vehicle access, particularly among low-income households that have traditionally supplied the region with its most frequent and reliable transit users."[62] The Bay Area Rapid Transit (BART) system has seen a moderate (but still slow) rebound in ridership since COVID-19, but that falling-ridership story is a consistent one across the state and throughout the country.[63] Only a few cities have seen sustained increases in transit use over time.

What to do when residents aren't hopping on the light-rail lines, buses, trolleys and commuter trains? There's the rub. Urbanists are so concerned about climate change and committed to ending suburbanization that they aren't willing to let consumer choice rule the day. They typically embrace policies that strike most of us as coercive.

One of those policies has been in place for decades and is so ubiquitous people rarely even notice it: the underinvestment in the transportation systems that most Americans rely upon to get around. That purposeful policy decision explains so much of our nation's congestion problem – and also leads to an unnecessary number of car-related deaths and injuries. California has, for instance, failed to seriously upgrade Highway 99, which cuts through the Central Valley. That's one reason it's known as the Freeway of Death.

A January study from the Rebuild SoCal Partnership found that "Infrastructure investment in Southern California has declined by 37 percent over the last decade" and "If Southern California were a state, it would rank 22nd in infrastructure investment and last in highway investments."[64] This isn't a new problem. One can find articles dating back to 1990 complaining about California's refusal to build and maintain the infrastructure needed to serve its once-growing population.[65] That's astounding when one considers that California in the 1960s was known for the quality of all types of infrastructure, from freeways to water systems to schools.

We can blame some of this on the usual bureaucratic nature of government, on the misallocation of resources and even on tax limitations (although I'd argue that there's always been plenty of money, but that the state has misspent it on other priorities). But some of it is intentional. While Gov. Pat Brown was known for spearheading the above-mentioned infrastructure expansion,[66] his son, Jerry, made the following remarks in his 1976 State of the State address:

> In short, we are entering an era of limits. In place of a manifest economic destiny, we face a sober reassessment of new economic realities; and we all have to get used to it. We can't ignore the demands of social and economic justice or the fragile environment on which we all depend. But, in meeting our responsibility, we are now forced to make difficult choices. Freeways, childcare, schools, income assistance, pensions, health programs, prisons, environmental protection – all must compete with one another and be subject to the careful scrutiny of the common purpose we all serve. It is a relentless test, one that the growing number of former democracies throughout the world have found they could not meet. It is now a question of reordering priorities and choosing one program over another based on a rigorous standard of equity and common sense. We should do those things which government does well, perform them in the most effective manner, and help those most in need.[67]

It's certainly true that state governments need to make hard choices, but largely since then the state has chosen not to make basic infrastructure a top priority and has used the ideology of limits as a highfalutin excuse. When Gov. Gray Davis announced the end of the era of freeway construction in the late 1990s, he touted the new way of focusing more on projects that reduced our car dependence. Since then, the state has spent far more proportionally on transit even though most Californians – including lower- and middle-income ones – continue to rely on their cars and car infrastructure.

An environmental ethos has long dominated California's policymaking, so the environmental movement's embrace of climate change has driven many of these priorities. Some environmental groups, such as the Natural Resources Defense Council, forthrightly call for reducing support for freeway and road construction.[68] Its recent report focused heavily on the downsides of automobiles, blaming climate pollution on "nearly a century of public investment totaling hundreds of billions of dollars in car-oriented transportation in the form of the state's sprawling freeway system and car-dependent communities."[69]

Car critics tend to have a muddled view of subsidies that fail to account for the modern transportation funding system that relies heavily on user fees paid by drivers. Cars are still subsidized via other taxes, but at a far lower rate than alternative public transportation systems. In fact, transit depends on subsidies from drivers.[70]

This push is bolstered by academic research that increasingly focuses solely on the negatives of driving. One recent academic study found that "people were significantly more likely to respond in what could be characterized as auto-centric attitudes. On the questions related to excusing negative externalities (i.e. rule-breaking, accepting consequences to society, and second-hand emissions), once again respondents were more likely to excuse negative car effects. By contrast, they were less likely to excuse second-hand smoke."[71] Well, yeah, people assess risks and are likely to downplay the risks of things that they depend upon in their daily lives.

We've also seen some unobjectionable policies morph into zealotry. Even car-dependent suburbanites such as myself generally welcome the construction of bicycle lanes, even if we wonder about their overall value given how unused they often are. But strident bike advocates aren't always content with the new lane investments, and sometimes even call them "murder lanes."[72] They now demand lanes that are segregated by concrete barriers. Some of their banter is silly, albeit illuminating, but it shows that for large segments of the urbanist population sensible half-measures that augment our current road system will never satisfy them. They seek a radical change in the design of our communities and transportation systems.

For now, the direct attacks on cars are easy to overlook. Modest efforts to limit road usage are annoying but pose no existential threat to our current system. No one is coming to take the keys to your Ford F-150. But there has been a successful war on driving that has slowly pulled back on infrastructure improvements. It hasn't reduced driving as much as it has increased congestion and the resulting misery, but it's safe to bet that these anti-car crusaders are eager to step up their activism.

Urbanism and the 'War' on Families

ONE OF THE LATEST fads from urbanists is to promote the construction of family-sized apartments in cities.73 It's an acknowledgement that rebuilding our society along more urbanized lines isn't attainable if people high-tail it to the suburbs as soon as they want to start a family. There are many reasons that young people eventually flee big cities, but the lack of availability of affordable, sufficiently sized homes certainly is one of them.

Vox's Rachel Cohen notes that Millennials "have accounted for more than half the population increase in 'close-in' urban neighborhoods in the country's largest metro areas since 2010, and they credit our migration (and our taxes) with accelerating urban revival. … But as they get older, the number of urban children has continued to drop. Lower birth rates are part of the story, but economists say the strong correlations with population shifts strongly suggest that 'out-migration' of cities explains a big portion of the loss. In other words, millennials now in their mid-30s and 40s with young kids have started decamping for suburbs to raise their families."[74]

Anecdotally, this doesn't appear to be anything new. When I was in my 20s living in Washington, D.C., my wife and I headed to the Maryland suburbs in preparation for the birth of our first daughter.

Many of our friends did the same thing. In fact, my daughter now is in her 30s, is expecting her first child and, sure enough, is planning an exit from her close-in San Francisco neighborhood. One of the driving forces is the lack of living space and the desire for a yard.

Cohen does a fair job discussing some of the policy proposals to promote more family housing. She writes about mandates that would force developers to include larger apartments in their mix. Fortunately, she quotes a land-use expert who makes the obvious point: dictating the product mix will increase development costs, could push these builders out of town and might reduce the overall number of apartments. She also touches on market-based ideas – reducing regulations that make it too costly to build bigger units (such as rules requiring two staircases in multifamily projects or large setbacks that eat up valuable floor space).[75] The latter ideas are reasonable ones.

I'd argue, however, that the real problem centers on demand. Cities remain a magnet for young, childless professionals. It's difficult to find larger apartments for families because most people don't want to raise their families in the city. It's not only about a dearth of spacious apartments, condos and houses, but about concerns with poor-performing school systems, crime issues and homeless encampments that have taken over neighborhood parks, and the high cost of living.

Ultimately, any effort to reduce suburban-living options will discourage people from having families. Anti-suburban policies that drive up home prices and reduce family oriented options are not a direct "war" on families, but an indirect one. Such policies ignore the natural and understandable needs of young families, especially those on tight budgets.

Urbanists often highlight the enormous cost of automobiles, with their monthly payments, insurance bills, and gas and maintenance costs.[76] But most families are capable of calculating the costs and benefits of alternative living arrangements. Cars are pricey, but everything else in bigger cities is generally costlier than in the suburbs – rent/mortgages, groceries, taxes, etc. When my wife and I considered moving into an urban area, we quickly learned that the local schools performed poorly. Private school tuition was far more than the cost of a second car.

As couples have children, their priorities shift. They worry less about walking to hip restaurants and bars – and more about neighborhood safety, educational opportunities and convenience. By failing to treat these concerns seriously and focusing instead on the availability of three-bedroom apartments, urbanists become their own worst enemy. The population numbers from major West Coast cities make it clear that fleeing for the suburbs is not an anomaly.

Most of the nation's biggest cities – and the ones usually touted by urbanists as models – are essentially childless. "San Francisco is not an easy place to raise kids. The city's soaring cost of living and large share of professionally oriented adults have contributed to making it the most childless city in the U.S. for years, behind other expensive urban hubs like New York and Seattle," according to a 2021 report in the *San Francisco Chronicle*.[77] Children make up only 13% of the city's population, compared to 22% of the nation's total population and 26% of its suburbs.[78]

Some of the population drop reflects overall lower birth rates throughout the country, but the exodus of families from cities continues. According to a study last year by the Economic Innovation Group, "Between July 1, 2020, and July 1, 2021, large urban counties – counties which intersect with an urban area of at least 250,000 people – experienced a sharp drop in their under-five population. After falling by more than 235,000 during that span (3.7%), this population fell an additional 106,000 last year, a drop of 1.8%."[79] The drop was most pronounced in the nation's biggest, elite cities.

There's much handwringing among urbanists about this phenomenon, but the reasons always end up centering on the obvious ones I raised above. Per a recent column in *The Conversation*: "Why are these families leaving large cities? There are many reasons, including high costs of living and housing, quality of education and school systems, crime and safety concerns and environmental and health factors."[80]

It's obvious, too, why many kids raised in somewhat sterile suburbs are eager to pursue opportunities in exciting urban environments, but it's wrong to assume that this age-old trend represents a permanent resurgence of big city living. It's even worse to use government planning to try to restrict people's choices. By making family friendly suburban living options less available, urbanists (at least the ones focused on mandates rather than up-zoning) are making it harder for young people to start families. I doubt that a boost in three-bedroom urban apartments will solve that problem.

Do Cities Subsidize Suburbs?

URBANISTS OFTEN JUSTIFY their anti-suburban policies based on a fairness issue. They argue that cities subsidize the suburbs and this shift of resources robs cities of their tax revenues and that leads to a decline in their quality of life. It's odd for a movement that eagerly supports public subsidies for, say, transit systems, parks and affordable-housing complexes to suddenly get upset about tax subsidies. Hypocrisy aside, what do the numbers suggest?

The suburban-subsidy argument takes a variety of shapes and forms, some of them nonsensical and others more or less accurate. The first argument is simple and wrongheaded. It goes like this: Low-density suburban development requires costly infrastructure to sustain it. By contrast, high-density living requires fewer roads and sewer lines, so general public revenues are misallocated by supporting single-family neighborhoods and sprawling commercial developments.

Here's how one urbanist, Kōrero Wellington, puts it:

> Suburban areas aren't just lower intensity in terms of homes and land-uses per hectare, they're also *lower*

revenue for their city. But they still need all the pipes, power, roads, footpaths, culverts, streetlamps, retaining walls and so on – all paid for by the city (i.e., the public – that's all of us). All the same costs, for many fewer people living, working, doing stuff per hectare. Suburbs are being propped up by the densely-populated, multi-use areas in the same city jurisdiction. It seems obvious when you think about it, but we generally don't.[81]

We can easily see the problem with this common argument based on the author's own words, as suburbs are "propped up" by the densely populated "areas in the same city." Most American suburbs – at least the ones in California – operate as independent cities.[82] In my suburb, taxpayers are paying for our infrastructure the same way as taxpayers in the neighboring big city pay for their infrastructure. There's no city-to-suburb subsidy here.

In fact, suburban tax rates are often lower than urban ones, as we have more efficient services thanks to less bureaucracy, fewer social-service programs, more-limited public spaces and less-powerful municipal unions. In some cases, suburbs – especially smaller, wealthier ones – have higher tax rates than neighboring cities, but the cities aren't subsidizing them. The suburban residents are paying them. Cities are sometimes net exporters of tax revenue to the state, although sometimes they are the recipient of more than their share.[83] Suburban Orange County, for instance, has long been a donor county.[84]

More sophisticated urbanists are forthright about the subsidy situation. Writer Chris Bradford spells it out in *Smart Cities Dive*:

There's not much direct subsidy of suburban subdivisions – developers pay for all interior roads and sidewalks, sewer and water hookups to city lines, and drainage and water retention facilities. They pay steep fees for city reviews and inspections. Depending on the size of the project, the city might require the developer to build on-site facilities like wastewater treatment plants. The city charges impact fees on top of these costs, and also can make developers pay the cost of off-site improvements that are roughly proportionate to the development's impact.[85]

Bradford's complaint is a reasonable one. He takes issue with the billions of dollars that county residents spend in bonds to fund arterial roads that support far-flung developments. However, every kind of infrastructure costs money, with the costs rarely paid fully by users. Wherever we live, we need to get around. Increased urbanization is predicated on the construction and expansion of transit systems. Users never pay the full freight for those.

Writing for the Cato Institute in 2018, Randal O'Toole argues that, "(W)e should end subsidies to highways as well, though those subsidies are much smaller – 1.5 cents per passenger mile vs. nearly 90 cents for transit."[86] So if subsidies are the urbanists' problem, we should look at who pays what for whom and recreate a tax system based on the principle that the user pays the costs. I'm guessing that with all costs considered, suburban residents would come out ahead.

That reality leads urbanists into a more fanciful definition of subsidies. *Grist* writer Ben Adler details one major federal "subsidy" for suburbia, the mortgage-interest deduction:

The nominal purpose of the deduction is to promote homeownership. What it actually does is promote the over-consumption of housing relative to other forms of spending, savings and investment, because it taxes a dollar spent on housing less than a dollar put elsewhere. … And that's not all. Over the same five-year period, homeowners wrote off $106 billion in federal income tax liability using rules that allow you to deduct state and local property taxes from your taxable income.[87]

Sorry, but I refuse to concede that allowing Americans to keep their own money is a subsidy even if, say, overall lower tax rates are generally better than targeted deductions. The mortgage and other tax deductions apply to any homeowner, including ones who purchase homes or condos in big cities. Urbanists also like to trot out supposed subsidies in the form of environmental externalities. In other words, the general public pays x for the health impacts of car dependency. Yet those imprecise numbers are generally a means to gin up costs to arrive at their pre-ordained conclusion. Anti-suburb types rarely insist on accounting for the environmental costs of transit and urban living.

In a 2017 *American Conservative* article, "How we subsidize suburbia," Devin Marisa Zuegel expands on the argument that federal policy drove suburban development: "By making long-term, amortized loans with low down payments the norm, federal policies made it possible for millions of people to buy single-family homes. These homeowners enthusiastically moved into the new mass-produced subdivisions to the west."[88]

Now tell me why this is a bad thing? It's not exactly a subsidy, either, by the common definition of that term. Of course, urbanists are right that other government policies, such as zoning and federal highway construction (paid for largely but not entirely by drivers through user fees), helped create the modern suburb. It was not, as some of suburbia's defenders claim, a miracle of the free-market system.

Zoning in particular is a government prior restraint on development, which is why effective urbanists are committed to reducing zoning restrictions so that developers can build whatever consumers want. But it's wrong – and generally inaccurate – to pit city residents against suburban ones by making it seem as if the former are subsidizing the latter. Simply put, urbanists would have far more success implementing the constructive aspects of their agenda if they described the situation accurately: Loosening building restrictions will lead to more choice and better outcomes for everyone. There's no need to make suburbs the scapegoat.

Conclusion: Seeking Peaceful Solutions

BEFORE SEARCHING FOR SOLUTIONS, it's wise to pinpoint the actual problem. Suburbia is not the problem. Cities are not the problem. The problem is a land-use process that's dominated by excessive government control. That results in housing shortages and soaring home prices. It results in a lack of freedom that limits our housing choices. Another genuine problem, which I frequently mention: Bureaucratic, incompetent and excessively priced municipal governments struggle to provide quality public services or to address problems that erode everyone's quality of life.[89] There's no magic formula, but we should reconsider our attitudes going forward.

It would be great for all of us to recognize that cities and their suburbs are not divided by something approximating the Berlin Wall. They are closely linked socially, economically and culturally. Big cities need suburban commuters just as suburbanites need urban job centers and amenities. Aaron Renn makes the requisite point in his *Governing* article, "Lies Cities Tell Themselves":

The truth is that a city and its suburbs are in a symbiotic relationship as part of an overall region. It's not the case that the suburbs are parasites on the city. Downtown is not just serving suburbanites, it's also dependent on them. Having major employers that people commute to is an asset, not a liability. Many major nonprofit institutions are likewise major assets and economic draws, not a burden.[90]

Maybe it sounds namby-pamby, but we should respect others' living choices and seek out conciliatory solutions whenever suburban and urban priorities run up against one another. City and county officials frequently work together on problems that cross municipal boundaries. That's nothing new even though there often are tensions. On a personal level, most of us enjoy our suburban communities, but frequently travel to the city and enjoy urban amenities. Many of our friends and relatives live in neighborhoods that differ greatly from our own.

New urbanists and YIMBYs in particular ought to knock off their cheap shots against suburbanites and explain to suburban dwellers why some mid-rise condos, better sidewalks and enhanced suburban downtowns might improve their quality of life and even boost home values. Critics of big cities – and there's an entire conservative cottage industry devoted to bashing San Francisco – should stop trading in dystopian imagery and support policies that improve the safety and livability of nearby cities.[91] You never know, your kids might end up choosing to live there. Many of the key urban and suburban governance issues aren't even partisan, so we should be open to areas of agreement.

This dispute might even open the doors to a needed debate about zoning. Most of the energy for reducing zoning comes from those who want to urbanize our land uses, but suburbia's conservative defenders might want to consider the reality of zoning in the context of their smaller-government political philosophy. In an interview with *Reason*, the late Bernie Siegan, author of "Land Use Without Zoning," spelled out zoning's inherent problems:

> When you give control to government you find that the process that's used by government is a process that really has nothing to do with the use of a valuable resource like land. In the case of land use, what you do is subject the use of land to the political process and political pressures, and when you do that the land will be used for reasons that have nothing to do with the optimum use of the land, with good planning (if I may use that term), and with any rational criteria for use of that land. Use will be determined by who has the political power, who has the graft, who has the influence, who has the multitude of things that causes the political powers to act as they do. I think that is counterproductive to the use of a very valuable resource.[92]

Moving decisions away from government planners, whether they are local, state or federal ones, would enhance freedom for everyone. Progressives who dominate the movement ought to apply this thinking more broadly – and not just to advance their particular end goals. Conservatives who oppose up-zoning reforms need to rediscover their first principles.

As far as specific public policies, I reiterate the importance of distinguishing between those that are indeed attacks on suburban life (e.g., growth controls) and those that simply allow suburban areas to change with the times (e.g., allowing higher densities). I'd like legislators to apply their streamlined, by-right development approaches to suburban developments, as well. Western states need more housing, so they might apply these liberalized rules to developers who build single-family homes, perhaps initially for smaller homes to encourage starter-house construction.

So is there a war on suburbia? Again, yes and no. Instead of trying to fight one, let's roll up our sleeves and engage in some peaceful mediation.

Endnotes

1   Parker, Kim. 2024. "What Unites and Divides Urban, Suburban and Rural Communities." Pew Research Center. April 14, 2024. https://www.pewresearch.org/social-trends/2018/05/22/what-unites-and-divides-urban-suburban-and-rural-communities/

2   Bloch, Matthew, Keith Collins, Robert Gebeloff, Marco Hernandez, Malika Khurana, and Zach Levitt. 2024. "Election Results Show a Red Shift Across the U.S. in 2024." *The New York Times*, November 21, 2024. https://www.nytimes.com/interactive/2024/11/06/us/politics/presidential-election-2024-red-shift.html.

3   Anderson, Jeffrey H. and Bureau of Justice Statistics. 2020. "Classification of Urban, Suburban, and Rural Areas in the National Crime Victimization Survey." Report NCJ 255923. *Bureau of Justice Statistics*. https://bjs.ojp.gov/content/pub/pdf/cusrancvs.pdf.

4   "Downtown Specific Plan." n.d. https://www.roseville.ca.us/government/departments/development_services/planning/specific_plans_planning_areas/downtown_specific_plan.

5   Vintage New Media, Inc. n.d. "Irvine - the Place to Be for High Rises."https://www.orangecountycondomania.com/article/Irvine-High-Rises.php.

6   Airgood-Obrycki, W. 2019. "Defining suburbs: How definitions shape the suburban landscape." Harvard University Joint Center for Housing Studies. https://www.jchs.harvard.edu/research-areas/working-papers/defining-suburbs-how-definitions-shape-suburban-landscape (Accessed: 14 December 2024).

7   Anderson, Jeffrey H. 2020. "Classification of Urban, Suburban, and Rural Areas in the National Crime Victimization Survey." Report NCJ 255923. Bureau of Justice Statistics. https://bjs.ojp.gov/content/pub/pdf/cusrancvs.pdf.

8   Whelan, Charlotte. 2020. "Joe Biden's War on Suburbia." Independent Women's Forum. July 22, 2020. https://www.iwf.org/2020/07/20/joe-bidens-war-on-suburbia/.

9   Ibid.

10 Trump, Donald, and Carson, Ben. 2020. "We'll protect America's suburbs." *The Wall Street Journal*. https://www.wsj.com/articles/well-protect-americas-suburbs-11597608133 (Accessed: 14 December 2024).

11 Cox, Wendell. 2024. "Large majority of U.S. minorities live in the suburbs." Pacific Research Institute. June 5, 2024. https://www.pacificresearch.org/large-majority-of-u-s-minorities-live-in-the-suburbs/#:~:text=Today%2C%20a%20majority%20of%20each,and%20exurbs%20(Figure%201).

12 Tobias, Manuela. 2022. "Duplex Housing Law Met With Fierce Resistance by California Cities." *CalMatters*, April 11, 2022. https://calmatters.org/housing/2022/04/duplex-housing-resistance/.

13 Gyselaar, Day. 2022. "American Suburbia: A Failed Experiment." *Medium*, January 5, 2022. https://medium.com/substance/american-suburbia-is-a-failed-experiment-3649918e6d1e.

14 Balashov, Alex. 2022. "Why Even Driving Through Suburbia Is Soul Crushing." *Quartz*, July 21, 2022. https://qz.com/698928/why-suburbia-sucks.

15 Hays, Gabriel. 2023. "Progressive Commentator Calls Out San Francisco as 'terrifying' 'nightmare': 'You're Going to Get Robbed.'" Fox News. October 28, 2023. https://www.foxnews.com/media/progressive-commentator-calls-san-francisco-terrifying-nightmare-youre-going-get-robbed.

16 Wamsley, Laurel. 2019. "Oregon Legislature Votes to Essentially Ban Single-Family Zoning." NPR, July 1, 2019. https://www.npr.org/2019/07/01/737798440/oregon-legislature-votes-to-essentially-ban-single-family-zoning.

17 Greenhut, Steven. 2023. "Don't Confuse 'Local Control' With Small Government." *Reason.com*, June 8, 2023. https://reason.com/2023/06/09/dont-confuse-local-control-with-small-government/.

18 Ibid.

19 Mai-Duc, Christine, and Parker, Will. "Why Private Developers Are Rejecting Government Money for Affordable Housing." *The Wall Street Journal.* www.wsj.com/real-estate/private-developers-affordable-housing-public-funds-3b779780.

20 Trump, Donald, and Carson, Ben, "We'll protect America's suburbs." *The Wall Street Journal.* https://www.wsj.com/articles/well-protect-americas-suburbs-11597608133 (Accessed: 14 December 2024).

21 Wintz, Levi. 2024. "Competing Against Suburbia." CNU. June 20, 2024. https://www.cnu.org/publicsquare/2024/06/30/competing-against-suburbia.

22 Garnett, Nicole Stelle. n.d. "Save the Cities, Stop the Suburbs?" *Yale Law Journal.* https://www.yalelawjournal.org/review/save-the-cities-stop-the-suburbs.

23 "Suburb." 2024. In *Merriam-Webster Dictionary.* https://www.merriam-webster.com/dictionary/suburb.

24 Greenhut, Steven. "Building Cities From Scratch." Pacific Research Institute. October 9, 2024. https://www.pacificresearch.org/building-cities-from-scratch/.

25 "Are You a Robot?" 2017. May 15, 2017. *Bloomberg.* https://www.bloomberg.com/news/articles/2017-05-15/how-gentrifying-neighborhoods-fall-short-on-diversity.

26   Mitchell, Travis. 2024. "1. Demographic and Economic Trends in Urban, Suburban and Rural Communities." Pew Research Center. April 14, 2024. https://www.pewresearch.org/social-trends/2018/05/22/demographic-and-economic-trends-in-urban-suburban-and-rural-communities/.

27   Weller, Chris. 2016. "There May Be an Evolutionary Reason Suburbia Feels so Miserable." *Business Insider.* September 15, 2016. https://www.businessinsider.com/why-suburbs-are-bad-2016-9.

28   Smith, Andrew. 2024. "An Ode to the Suburb." Pacific Research Institute. January 5, 2024. https://www.pacificresearch.org/an-ode-to-the-suburb/.

29   "The Rise of Suburbs | US History II (American Yawp)." n.d. https://courses.lumenlearning.com/suny-ushistory2ay/chapter/the-rise-of-suburbs-2/.

30   Ibid.

31   "What Is Smart Growth?" 2023. Smart Growth America. August 8, 2023. https://smartgrowthamerica.org/what-is-smart-growth/.

32   Terrain.org. 2020. "Successional Urbanism: Interview with Andrés Duany." June 15, 2020. https://www.terrain.org/2013/interviews/andres-duany/.

33   "The Story of Seaside, Florida." 2024. SoWal.com. July 11, 2024. https://sowal.com/story/the-story-of-seaside-florida.

34 Terrain.org. 2020. "Successional Urbanism: Interview With Andrés Duany." June 15, 2020. https://www.terrain.org/2013/interviews/andres-duany/.

35 Ibid.

36 Delgado, Carla. 2021. "Is City Living Bad for Your Health?" *Discover* Magazine. November 9, 2021. https://www.discover-magazine.com/health/is-city-living-bad-for-your-health.

37 Del Mastro, Addison. 2019. "An Interview with James Howard Kunstler." *The American Conservative*. November 13, 2019. https://www.theamericanconservative.com/an-interview-with-james-howard-kunstler/.

38 Bannon, Jim. 1999. "The geography of nowhere." *Mountain Xpress*. December 13, 2024. https://mountainx.com/news/community-news/0922kunstler-php/.

39 McLean, Danielle. 2022. "Converting Strip Malls Into Mixed-use Development Could Address California's Housing Crisis." *Smart Cities Dive*, April 27, 2022. https://www.smartcitiesdive.com/news/converting-strip-malls-mixed-use-development-california-housing-crisis/622643/.

40 "UGB 101: Everything You Wanted to Know About the Urban Growth." 2020. Metro. January 16, 2020. https://www.oregonmetro.gov/news/ugb-101-everything-you-wanted-know-about-urban-growth-boundary-were-afraid-ask.

41   ACT Government; Land Release to Enable More Than 21,000 New Homes for Canberrans." Chief Minister, Treasury and Economic Development Directorate. https://www.cmtedd.act. gov.au/open_government/inform/act_government_media_re-leases/chris-steel-mla-media-releases/2024/land-release-to-enable-more-than-21,000-new-homes-for-canberrans.

42   Beyer, Scott. 2017. "Portland's Urban Growth Boundary: A Driver of Suburban Sprawl." *Forbes*, March 30, 2017. https://www.forbes.com/sites/scottbeyer/2017/03/29/portlands-ur-ban-growth-boundary-a-driver-of-suburban-sprawl/.

43   Staff. 2024. "Does It Take You Over an Hour to Get to Work? Stanford Study Looks at 'Super Commuters'." NBC Bay Area, June 5, 2024. https://www.nbcbayarea.com/news/local/stan-ford-super-commuters-study/3557477/.

44   Bütow, Roger E. 2024. "CEQA-Exempt SB-4, SB-9, SB-10: Will Coastal Cities Suffer the Most?" *Laguna Beach, CA Patch*, July 24, 2024. https://patch.com/california/lagunabeach/ceqa-exempt-sb-4-sb-9-sb-10-will-coastal-cities-suffer-most.

45   Kang, Ouyang. 2024. "California's ADU Opportunities in 2024." *LiveLarge Blog*. November 23, 2024. https://livelarge-tech.com/blog/adu-sustainability/unlock-your-propertys-po-tential-1-californias-adu-opportunities/.

46   Ring, Edward 2020. "California's Progressive War on Sub-urbia. California Policy Center." *California Policy Center Blog*. February 20, 2020. https://californiapolicycenter.org/californi-as-progressive-war-on-suburbia/.

47   Ibid.

48   Stevens, Harry. 2024. "How Walkable Is Your Neighbor-hood? Use Our Interactive Map to Find Out." *The Washington Post*. December 7, 2024. https://www.washingtonpost.com/climate-environment/interactive/2024/walkable-neighbor-hoods-suburban-sprawl-pollution/.

49   Kopecky, Karen and Suen, Ming Hon. University of Rochester. 2004. "Suburbanization and the Automobile." https://users.nber.org/~confer/2005/UEs05/kopecky.pdf.

50   Ibid.

51   "Are You Suffering From Advanced Car Brain?" 2022. *Planning Blog*. August 28, 2022. https://colinhunter.net/2022/05/12/are-you-suffering-from-advanced-car-brain/.

52   "Stats of the States - Accident Mortality." U.S. Centers for Disease Control. n.d. https://www.cdc.gov/nchs/pressroom/sosmap/accident_mortality/accident.htm.

53   Greenhut, Steven. 2024. Pacific Research Institute. "State Planners Focus Too Much on Social Engineering Rather Than Transportation Engineering." February 27, 2024. https://www.pacificresearch.org/new-pri-book-state-planners-focus-too-much-on-social-engineering-rather-than-transportation-engineering/.

54   Pendall, Rolf. 2014. "For Many Low-income Families, Cars May Be Key to Greater Opportunity." Urban Institute. April 1, 2014. https://www.urban.org/urban-wire/many-low-in-come-families-cars-may-be-key-greater-opportunity.

55 Monbiot, George. 2019. "Cars Are Killing Us. Within 10 Years, We Must Phase Them Out." *The Guardian*, March 7, 2019. https://www.theguardian.com/commentisfree/2019/mar/07/cars-killing-us-driving-environment-phase-out.

56 Frearson, Amy. 2022. "Berlin Citizens Propose Law to Ban Cars From City Centre." *Dezeen*, February 9, 2022. https://www.dezeen.com/2022/01/28/car-free-berlin-autofrei/.

57 Staff. 2024. "Germany Considers Banning Weekend Driving to Meet Climate Goals." *The European Conservative*, April 15, 2024. https://europeanconservative.com/articles/news/germany-considers-banning-weekend-driving-to-meet-climate-goals/.

58 Richter, Konstantin. 2024. "Germany's car industry is losing its famous Vorsprung – and it can't all be blamed on Trump and tariffs." *The Guardian*, November 14, 2024. https://www.theguardian.com/commentisfree/2024/nov/14/germany-car-industry-donald-trump-tariffs.

59 Greenhut, Steven. 2019. "Your Tax Dollars at Work as Cities Shut Traffic Lanes." *The Orange County Register*. June 1, 2019. https://www.ocregister.com/2019/06/01/your-tax-dollars-at-work-as-cities-shut-traffic-lanes/.

60 Lazo, Alejandro. 2024. "Supreme Court to Weigh in on Case Involving California's Power to Clean Its Air." *CalMatters*, December 13, 2024. https://calmatters.org/environment/2024/12/supreme-court-california-vehicle-emission-standards/#:~:text=The%20regulation%2C%20known%20as%20California's,have%20zero%20emissions%20by%202035.

61 Gupta, Mehul. 2023. "Electric Vehicles Are Not the Solution. Sustainable Transit Is." *Chicago Policy Review*. March 30, 2023. https://chicagopolicyreview.org/2023/04/04/electric-vehicles-are-not-the-solution-sustainable-transit-is/.

62 Chu, Tiffany, Ryan Kurtzman, Joseph Marynak, Trevor Thomas, University of California Institute of Transportation Studies Mobility Research Program, Southern California Association of Governments, and United States Department of Transportation. January 2018. "Falling Transit Ridership: California And Southern California." https://scag.ca.gov/sites/main/files/file-attachments/its_scag_transit_ridership.pdf.

63 Staff, BER. 2024. "A Slow Speed Recovery: BART's Troublesome Post-Pandemic Comeback." March 13, 2024. https://econreview.studentorg.berkeley.edu/a-slow-speed-recovery-barts-troublesome-post-pandemic-comeback/.

64 Rebuild SoCal Partnership and Blue Sky Consulting Group. March 2024. "The High Cost Of Underinvestment: Assessing The State of Infrastructure in Southern California." https://rebuild2024.wpenginepowered.com/wp-content/uploads/2024/03/2024-RebuildSoCal-Infrastructure-Report-1.pdf.

65 Trombley, William. 1990. "California in State of Fast Decay : The Infrastructure Is Crumbling After Years of Neglect. But It's Difficult to See Where the Billions for Repairs and New Facilities Will Come From." *Los Angeles Times*. February 11, 1990. https://www.latimes.com/archives/la-xpm-1990-02-11-mn-1020-story.html.

66 Climate-Safe Infrastructure Working Group, OPR Office of Planning and Research, J.R. Gibson, Gordon, Beale, Little Hoover

Commission, E. Hanak, et al. n.d. "Milestones in California Infrastructure Thinking, Planning and Policy-Making." https://resources.ca.gov/CNRALegacyFiles/docs/climate/ab2800/Appendix12_Milestones_FINAL.pdf.

67 California State Library. n.d. "Governors of California - Edmund G. Brown Jr. State of the State Address." https://governors.library.ca.gov/addresses/s_34-JBrown1.html.

68 "Environmental Groups Challenge Highway Expansion Project in Court." October 17, 2024. https://www.nrdc.org/press-releases/environmental-groups-challenge-highway-expansion-project-court.

69 Rubin, Carter, Abonour, Rabi, Gahbauer, John. 2023. Natural Resources Defense Council. "Closing The Climate Investment Gap: California Must Prioritize Climate-Smart Transportation Projects." https://www.nrdc.org/sites/default/files/2023-09/ca-transportation-investment-report.pdf.

70 California Legislative Analyst's Office, "FAQs." https://lao.ca.gov/Transportation/FAQs. Accessed December 14, 2024.

71 Goddard, Tara. 2024. "Windshield Bias, Car Brain, Motornormativity: Different Names, Same Obscured Public Health Hazard." https://doi.org/10.32866/001c.122974.

72 Greenhut, Steven 2023. "Sorry, Urbanists, but Bicycles Will Never Save the Planet." *The Orange County Register.* November 10, 2023. https://www.ocregister.com/2023/11/10/sorry-urbanists-but-bicycles-will-never-save-the-planet/.

73 Justus, Andrew, and Andrew Justus. 2023. "How to Build More Family-sized Apartments." *Niskanen Center - Improving Policy, Advancing Moderation Blog.* January 9, 2023. https://www.niskanencenter.org/how-to-build-more-family-sized-apartments/.

74 Cohen, Rachel. 2023. "Where Are All the Apartments for Families?" *Vox*, April 23, 2023. https://www.vox.com/policy/2023/4/23/23686130/housing-apartments-family-yimby-nimby-zoning-suburbs.

75 Ibid.

76 Gardner, Charlie. "Auto Costs and Housing Costs, or, One Reason the Suburbs Are so Appealing." *Old Urbanist Blogspot.* March 2015. https://oldurbanist.blogspot.com/2015/03/auto-costs-and-housing-costs-or-one.html.

77 Neilson, Susie. 2021. "Is San Francisco the Most Childless City in the Country? Here's a Look at the Data on Kids." *San Francisco Chronicle*, August 14, 2021. https://www.sfchronicle.com/sf/article/Is-San-Francisco-still-losing-kids-Here-s-what-16383942.php.

78 Livingston, Gretchen. 2024. "Family Life Is Changing in Different Ways Across Urban, Suburban and Rural Communities in the U.S." Pew Research Center, April 14, 2024. https://www.pewresearch.org/short-reads/2018/06/19/family-life-is-changing-in-different-ways-across-urban-suburban-and-rural-communities-in-the-u-s/.

79 Sandhovel, Amelia. 2024. "Young Families Have Not Returned to Large Cities Post-Pandemic." Economic Innovation Group. January 7, 2024. https://eig.org/2023-family-exodus/.

80 Das, Biswa. 2024. "Young Families Are Leaving Many Large US Cities - Here's Why That Matters." *The Conversation.* November 20, 2024. https://theconversation.com/young-families-are-leaving-many-large-us-cities-heres-why-that-matters-238538#:~:text=During%20the%20COVID%2D19%20pandemic,Francisco%2C%20Los%20Angeles%20and%20Chicago.

81 Wellington, Kōrero. 2022. "Suburbia Is Subsidised: Here's the Maths." *Talk Wellington.* https://talkwellington.org.nz/2022/suburbia-is-subsidised-heres-the-maths/.

82 Carney, Kristen. 2024. "California Cities by Population." June 20, 2024. https://www.california-demographics.com/cities_by_population.

83 Renn, Aaron M. 2023. "Lies Cities Tell Themselves." *Governing.* February 23, 2023. https://www.governing.com/community/lies-cities-tell-themselves.

84 "Mission & History | OCTax." OCTax. https://www.octax.org/mission-history#:~:text=In%201992%2C%20OCTax%20unsuccessfully%20opposed,the%20rest%20of%20the%20state. Accessed December 14, 2024.

85 "How We Subsidize Suburban Growth by Providing the Roads It Requires." *Smart Cities Dive.* n.d. https://www.smartcitiesdive.com/ex/sustainablecitiescollective/we-really-do-subsidize-suburban-growth/30831/. Accessed December 14, 2024.

86 O'Toole, Randal. 2018. "Why We Need to Stop Subsidizing Public Transit." The Cato Institute. May 7, 2018. https://www.cato.org/commentary/why-we-need-stop-subsidizing-public-transit.

87 Adler, Ben, 2013. "Starving the Cities to Feed the Suburbs." *Grist*. January 9, 2013. https://grist.org/cities/starving-the-cities-to-feed-the-suburbs/.

88 Zuegel, Devon Marisa. 2020. "How We Subsidize Suburbia." *The American Conservative*. November 2, 2020. https://www.theamericanconservative.com/we-have-always-subsidized-suburbia/.

89 Knight, Heather. 2024. "San Francisco Tried to Build a $1.7 Million Toilet. It's Still Not Done." *The New York Times*. January 24, 2024. https://www.nytimes.com/2024/01/24/us/san-francisco-toilet.html.

90 Renn, Aaron M. 2023. "Lies Cities Tell Themselves." *Governing*. February 23, 2023. https://www.governing.com/community/lies-cities-tell-themselves.

91 Marcus, David. 2024. "Kamala Harris' San Francisco Is a Dystopian Nightmare. Is This What She Has Planned for America?" Fox News. August 17, 2024. https://www.foxnews.com/opinion/kamala-harris-san-francisco-dystopian-nightmare-what-she-has-planned-america.

92 Chase, Dennis. 2020. "The New Approach to Planning - Non-zoning." *Reason*. May 14, 2020. https://reason.com/1973/04/01/the-new-approach-to-planningno/.

About the Author

STEVEN GREENHUT is a longtime journalist who has covered California politics since 1998. He wrote this book for the San Francisco-based Pacific Research Institute, where he founded that think tank's Sacramento-based journalism center in 2009. He currently is western region director for the R Street Institute, a Washington, D.C.-based free-market think tank, and is on the editorial board of the Southern California News Group. Greenhut has worked fulltime as a columnist for the *Orange County Register* and the *San Diego Union-Tribune*. He writes weekly for *American Spectator* and *Reason* magazines. He is the editor of *Saving California*, and the author of *Winning the Water Wars, Abuse of Power* and *Plunder*. He is also the author of the Free Cities Center booklets *Back from Dystopia: A New Vision for Western Cities, Putting Customers First: Re-Envisioning our Approach to Transportation Planning,* and *Giving Housing Supply a Boost: How to Improve Affordability and Reduce Homelessness* (with Dr. Wayne Winegarden).

About Pacific Research Institute

The Pacific Research Institute (PRI) champions freedom, opportunity, and personal responsibility by advancing free-market policy solutions. It provides practical solutions for the policy issues that impact the daily lives of all Americans, and demonstrates why the free market is more effective than the government at providing the important results we all seek: good schools, quality health care, a clean environment, and a robust economy.

Founded in 1979 and based in San Francisco, PRI is a non-profit, non-partisan organization supported by private contributions. Its activities include publications, public events, media commentary, community leadership, legislative testimony, and academic outreach.

Center for Business and Economics

PRI shows how the entrepreneurial spirit—the engine of economic growth and opportunity—is stifled by onerous taxes, regulations, and lawsuits. It advances policy reforms that promote a robust economy, consumer choice, and innovation.

Center for Education

PRI works to restore to all parents the basic right to choose the best educational opportunities for their children. Through research and grassroots outreach, PRI promotes parental choice in education, high academic standards, teacher quality, charter schools, and school-finance reform.

Center for the Environment

PRI reveals the dramatic and long-term trend toward a cleaner, healthier environment. It also examines and promotes the essential ingredients for abundant resources and environmental quality: property rights, markets, local action, and private initiative.

Center for Health Care

PRI demonstrates why a single-payer Canadian model would be detrimental to the health care of all Americans. It proposes market-based reforms that would improve affordability, access, quality, and consumer choice.

Center for California Reform

The Center for California Reform seeks to reinvigorate California's entrepreneurial self-reliant traditions. It champions solutions in education, business, and the environment that work to advance prosperity and opportunity for all the state's residents.

Center for Medical Economics and Innovation

The Center for Medical Economics and Innovation aims to educate policymakers, regulators, health care professionals, the media, and the public on the critical role that new technologies play in improving health and accelerating economic growth.

Free Cities Center

The Free Cities Center cultivates innovative ideas to improve our cities and urban life based around freedom and property rights – not government.

www.ingramcontent.com/pod-product-compliance
Lightning Source LLC
Chambersburg PA
CBHW070030030426
42335CB00017B/2369